Have you ever been on a train?

I like playing with our railway set.

Sometimes I use straight pieces of track.

Sometimes I use curved pieces of track.

6

Which is the shortest way for my train to get to the station?

7

Sometimes I use a
diagram to help me
lay out my track.

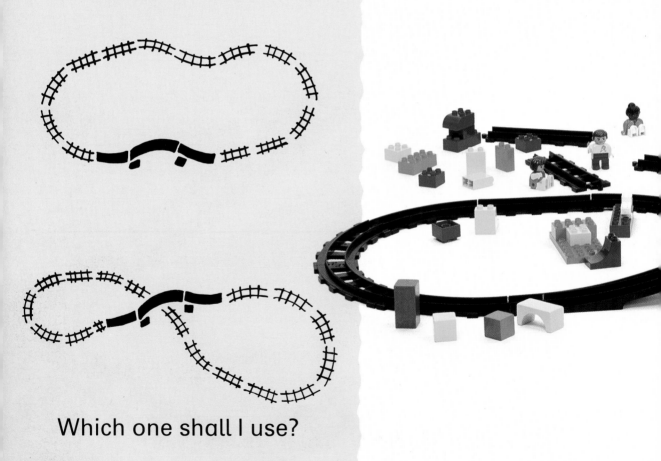

Which one shall I use?

Can you tell which diagram I chose?

Ben is making a long train, with three trucks and an engine.

Ben's train cannot go all the way along this track. Do you know why?

Katie is building a factory.

Ben is making a block of flats.

Katie and Ben are building
towns and villages.

The towns are joined
by railway track.

15

I'm drawing our towns and railway.

16

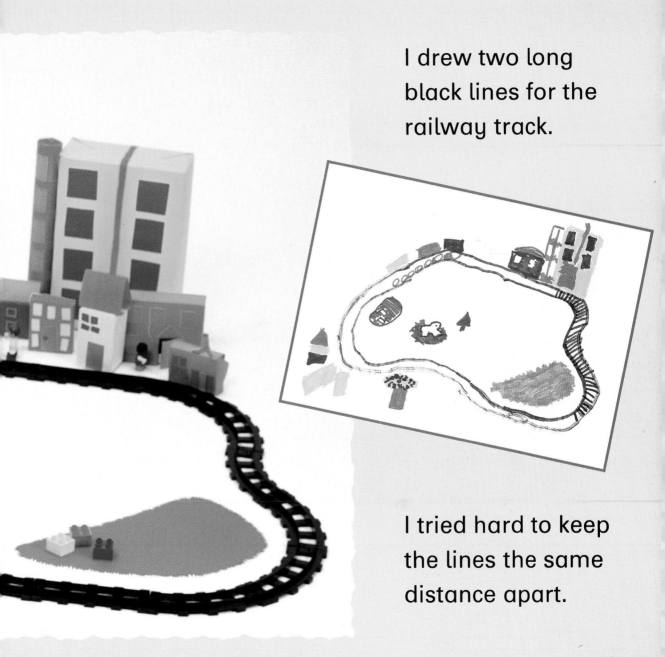

I drew two long black lines for the railway track.

I tried hard to keep the lines the same distance apart.

17

Katie is making a bridge for people to cross over the railway track.

18

Do you think the train will
fit under the bridge?

Can you think of
another way to
make a footbridge?

19

I'm making a tunnel for
the train to go through.

Can you think of another way
to make a tunnel?

Sometimes we
pretend we are
on a train.

I'm making
some tickets.

23

More things to do

1. Long and short tracks
Choose two places to be stations and lay a railway track between them. First, make the track as short as you can. What kind of pieces do you need? Next, make the track as long as you can. How many pieces of track have you used?

2. Looking for lines
Look all around you to see what sorts of lines you can find. Look for straight lines and curved lines. Can you find any lines which stay the same distance apart? These are called parallel lines. Make a list or draw some pictures of the lines you see.

3. Building with boxes
Here is one way to make flats and houses from old cardboard boxes. Cover the box with coloured paper by gluing pieces of paper to the front and sides. Cut out a rectangle of paper for the door and other shapes for the windows. Make sure the door is slightly bigger than any play-people you have. Make a roof from a piece of card folded in half. Fix the roof to the box with sticky tape. Draw window frames and drain pipes with a felt pen.

4. Railway truck painting
You can use a plastic railway truck to print parallel lines. Put some poster paint on a plate. Gently roll your truck through the paint to cover the edges of the wheels. Lean your paper on a magazine or some newspaper. Roll the truck over your paper, pressing down carefully. When you have finished, remember to wash the truck properly.

Find the page

This list shows you where to find some of the ideas in this book.

Notes for parents and teachers

As you read this book with children, these notes will help you to explain the mathematical ideas behind the different activities.

Real trains and model trains   pages 2, 3, 4

A visit to a railway station could be a useful introduction to the activities in this book. Talk about the similarities and differences between a model railway and the real thing.

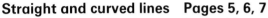

Straight and curved lines   Pages 5, 6, 7

A straight line is the shortest distance between two points, so the quickest way from one station to another is along the straight track. Talk about why real railway track does not always go in a straight line, for example, to avoid a hill or a lake.

Some children may be confident enough to measure the distance between different places on a model railway track with lengths of string or a tape measure.

Using diagrams   Pages 8, 9, 14, 15, 16, 17

A model railway is a representation of a real railway on a small scale and in a simplified form. The diagram is a two-dimensional representation of a three-dimensional model. It can take some time for young children to see the link between the diagram and the model.

Real railways do not usually run in a loop, allowing the train to travel back to where it started. Layouts which connect places, with complete towns at the beginning and end of each track are more realistic. Some children may be ready to draw their own simple diagrams, copying a layout they have made.

Right angles   Pages 10, 11

A train cannot go round a sharp bend or a right angle. To enable the train to change direction, the railway line is arranged in lengths of curved and straight track.

Building   Pages 12, 13, 14, 15, 18, 19, 20, 21

A combination of plastic construction materials, wooden bricks and cardboard gives children a great deal of scope for building. The railway track provides a context for their work.

Building models uses a variety of skills and concepts, including counting, comparing, measuring and estimating. Symmetry and pattern are often important, too. Children can use trial and improvement to make their buildings stronger, more interesting or better suited to their purposes. The idea of scale begins to develop, too.

Encourage children to be more observant about the buildings around them, and to use them as a source of ideas for their own model-building.

Position and direction   Pages 14, 15, 18, 19, 20, 21, 23

Some children will be ready to use words which describe position, such as over, under, through, next to, to and from. And some can talk about direction, using the words north and south.

Parallel lines   Pages 16, 17

The long rails of railway track are fixed so that they stay the same distance apart, to match the wheels of a train. Often, children think that parallel means the same as next to. Look out for other sets of parallel lines, such as those on regular stripes and ladders.